Contents

About netball

Netball is a fast, exciting team sport. It is played in many countries throughout the world. It is an easy game to play, but at a higher level becomes a very **tactical** game that needs great skill. It can be played by women and men of all ages and abilities, but at the moment many more women play than men. Usually women and men play in separate teams except when playing for fun. Junior school teams are also sometimes mixed (girls and boys).

How it all began

The original game was invented in America in 1891. At that time it was called basketball. It was introduced into England by a visiting American, Dr Toles, in 1895. The rules changed gradually until 1897, when the game was named netball. Since then, netball has grown in popularity.

The flags of some of the competing countries in the 1995 World Championships.

Organization

Within each country, netball is controlled and organized by a netball association. In England this is the All-England Netball Association (AENA). Wales, Scotland, Northern Ireland, Australia, New Zealand, South Africa and many other countries have their own netball associations.

The first international matches were played in 1949 when England, Scotland and Wales competed against each other. Soon other countries started to play international matches but each country had slightly different rules. To solve this problem, all the netball associations met in 1956 and agreed a common set of rules. They also formed a new body to coordinate netball throughout the world. This body is called the International Federation of Netball Associations (IFNA). There are currently 40 countries that are members of IFNA.

Major events

Every four years a big international netball tournament is held. This is called the World Championship. The first World Championship was held in Eastbourne, England, in 1963 with 11 countries competing. The ninth World Championship was held in Birmingham in 1995 and 27 countries competed. Netball is also included in the World Games. This is held every four years for non-Olympic sports. In 1998, netball will be included for the first time in the Commonwealth Games. So it is an exciting time for all netball enthusiasts.

Action from an under 16s' home international between England and Northern Ireland.

NETBALL FACTS

Netball is an *amateur* sport so players do not get paid. That means that the players play for the love of the sport rather than for money!

Playing the game

Netball is a game of passing played by two teams of seven players, on a rectangular court. The aim of the game is to score more **goals** than the other team. A goal is scored by shooting the ball through a metal hoop attached to the top of a post. A goal can only be scored from within the **goal circle**, so each team must get the ball into the circle before taking a shot at goal. This is done by passing the ball from player to player. Each player on the team is allowed only in certain areas of the court. It takes a team effort to move the ball from one end of the court to the other and to score a goal.

The court

Netball can be played indoors or outdoors on a hard surface. The court is 30.5 m by 15.25 m (100 ft by 50 ft). It is divided into thirds by two lines running across the width of the court. These are called **transverse lines**. At each end of the court there is a **goal post**, 3.05 m (10 ft) high with a metal hoop of 380 mm (15 in) in diameter. The goal circle is the area inside the semi-circle that is 4.9 m (16 ft) away from the goal post.

The layout and dimensions of a netball court.

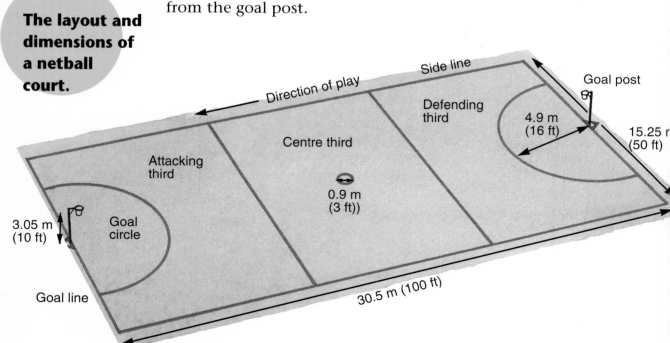

These players have their names on their shirts and their playing positions attached with velcro.

In the centre of the court is a circle, 0.9 m (3 ft) in diameter. This is called the **centre circle**. At the start of the game or after each goal is scored the game is restarted by a **centre pass** from this circle. The centre pass alternates between the two teams throughout the game.

Equipment

To play netball each player needs appropriate sports kit. This usually includes a suitable pair of shoes, a t-shirt, and skirt for women or shorts for men. For a match, players on the same team usually wear the same type and colour of kit. Each team needs a set of **playing bibs** to indicate each player's position. These need to be a different colour from the opposition so that players and **umpires** can see which team the player is on. Finally, no game would be possible without the ball. This should be a size 5 netball. The ball is the same size and weight as a soccer ball but the surface is different. The surface of a netball is rougher to help players grip it.

NETBALL FACTS

Most international teams no longer wear playing bibs. Instead they attach their playing positions to their shirts with Velcro or press-studs. Many also have the player's name across the top of their shirts, as shown in the picture.

Positions and roles

A netball squad is usually made up of ten players. Only seven players are allowed on court at one time. The other three players are called substitutes. Each player on court has a specific playing position and plays within certain areas of the court. The seven playing positions are Goal Shooter (GS), Goal Attack (GA), Wing Attack (WA), Centre (C), Wing Defence (WD), Goal Defence (GD) and Goal Keeper (GK). The areas where each player is allowed are shown in the diagram.

Playing positions

The playing positions can be divided into three groups: the **shooters** (GS, GA), the **centre court players** (WA, C, WD) and the **defenders** (GD, GK).

Shooters

The shooters' main job is to score **goals**! Both shooters need to be accurate and to be able to catch any missed shots. These are called rebounds. The GS must be able to take up a good position in the **goal circle** and have good ball-handling skills to receive a pass. The GA has to help the WA receive **centre passes** and bring the ball towards the circle. The GS and GA work together to get the ball into the circle and shoot. It helps a lot if shooters are tall and mobile because then defenders find it hard to defend the shot.

The blue parts of the court show the playing areas for each of the seven playing positions.

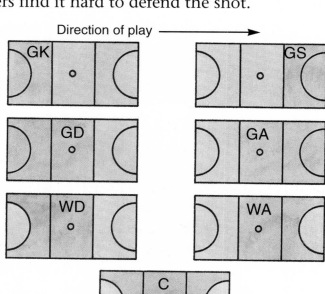

Direction of play ⟶

Centre court players

The centre court players work together to bring the ball from the defenders to the shooters. The C's main roles are to give centre passes and attack or defend from one goal circle to the other. The WA must try to catch the centre passes and feed the ball into the shooters' area. If the opposition gets the ball, the WA must help defend and try to win the ball back.

The WD's main role is to prevent the opposing WA from receiving the ball and passing it up the court towards the shooters. When the defence has made an **interception**, the WD must attack back down the court. The centre court players all need speed, mobility and accuracy in passing.

Defenders

The defenders' main aim is to stop the opposing shooters from getting the ball into the goal circle and scoring. This requires defensive skills such as **marking a player** and intercepting the ball. When a shooter misses a shot, the defenders must be able to get the rebound, then link with the WD to start an attacking move back down the court. As with the shooters, it helps to be a tall defender.

In this picture, the red Centre has just taken the centre pass and the Goal Attack is about to receive the ball.

Passing and receiving

In netball, a player cannot move far with the ball, so it has to be moved about the court by passing. That is why passing is one of the main skills of the game. To score a **goal** a team must first pass the ball along the court to the **goal circle**. There are a number of different techniques for passing the ball.

Which pass to use?

This depends on how far away the player is and where the **defender** is. Three passes are described below but there are others including the lob, the hip pass and the under-arm pass.

The **shoulder pass** is a fast, hard pass used over long distances. It is a one-handed pass and the ball is thrown from shoulder or head height. If a player is throwing the ball with the right hand, the left foot should be forward to help the player balance. For a left-hand throw, the right foot is forward.

When passing over a shorter distance a player can use a **chest pass**. This is a two-handed pass thrown from the chest of the thrower towards the chest of the receiver. As with all passes, the player extends the arms in the direction of the pass and **follows through**.

A **bounce pass** is a low pass that is also used over a short distance. The ball is pushed towards the ground with either one or two hands. It should reach the receiver between knee and waist level. The bounce pass is useful for passing round a tall defender or passing to a **shooter** in the goal circle.

When a player receives the ball they must control it, get ready to throw it and make a pass. Players are only allowed to hold the ball for three seconds. During this time the player must also decide whom to pass the ball to, when to pass and where. There is a lot to think about!

Whom to pass to?

This depends on the direction of play, which players are free and where their opponents are. Players should try to pass the ball in the direction of the goal. If a player cannot pass forward, a pass sideways or backwards may be made.

When to pass?

This depends on two things: how long it takes the thrower to make the pass and the movements of the player who is to receive the ball.

Where to pass?

Players should pass into a space that the receiver can reach before the defender. If the receiver is running, the ball should be thrown into the space in front. If the receiver is standing still with a defender to one side, the ball should be passed into the space on the other side.

The player on the left has just thrown a chest pass and demonstrates a good follow-through position.

POINTERS

The follow-through is the extension of the arms, hands and fingers as the ball is released. The players step onto the front foot at the same time. This all helps give the ball direction.

Shooting

The final ball movement in a successful attack is a shot at **goal**. Of the seven players on a team only two can shoot – the Goal Shooter (GS) and Goal Attack (GA). When a team has worked hard to get the ball into its **goal circle** it expects the **shooters** to score. It does not matter how good the rest of the team is – if the shooters are not scoring then the team will not win! This puts a lot of pressure on the shooters. Shooters need to be very calm and confident. Any nerves or lack of confidence might interfere with the players' shooting action. However, when the GS or GA is shooting well they get a lot of the glory.

South Africa's Irene Van Dyk shoots for goal.

Shooting action

There are many different types of shooting action but they have some basic factors in common. As for passing, it is important for the player to be balanced. This means having the feet apart. The ball should be held as high as possible. This will make it harder for the **defender** to reach. The fingers of the shooting hand are spread under the ball and point backwards. The other hand is at the side of the ball to help control it. As the player prepares to shoot, they bend the arms and legs. Then they extend upwards through the legs and arms and **follow through**. The ball is released from as high a point as possible. The flight of the ball should be high so that the ball can drop through the ring more easily.

Tall players

Being a tall shooter has its advantages. It makes it harder for defenders to mark the shot and to get rebounds. Sometimes smaller defenders can jump higher than a tall shooter so it balances out. At the 1995 World Championship, Irene Van Dyk from South Africa made a big impression. At 190 cm (6 ft 4 in) tall she was not the tallest shooter but she could jump! Defenders from all opposing teams found it very difficult to stop Irene receiving the ball!

NETBALL FACTS

At the 1995 World Championship, Angela Maoate of the Cook Islands had the highest shooting average, scoring 90.2 per cent of the shots she attempted. Irene Van Dyk of South Africa was close behind with an average of 90 per cent. She also scored the most goals in total: 543 goals in ten games!

Jennifer Borlase (GS) has created space to receive the ball in the goal circle.

Attacking

During a game, players make many different movements to try to win the ball and score **goals**. These movements can be divided into **attacking** movements and **defending** movements. Attacking movements are made by players when their team has the ball. There are strict rules about the movements of a player who is holding the ball.

Footwork

When a player catches the ball in the air, the first foot to touch the ground is called the landing foot. This foot can be used as a pivot while the player moves the second foot. The player can step onto the second foot but must throw the ball before replacing the landing foot again. This means a player cannot travel far with the ball. It does not mean players have to stop with the ball. Skilled players can receive and release the ball while moving very fast, without breaking the footwork rule.

Good footwork is not just about the footwork rules. It is important for balance and control in all movements.

The blue Goal Attack is getting free by sprinting away from the opposing Goal Defence.

Getting free

Attacking players must move into a position where they can receive the ball and pass it on to another player. This is called **getting free**. There are a number of different ways of getting free. A player can sprint away from an opponent into a space to receive a pass. A player can run one way then suddenly change direction and run another way. A player who is standing still can use a **feint dodge**. This is when a player pretends to move in one direction (a feint) but suddenly goes in the other direction.

One method that is used a lot by **shooters** is called **holding a space**. The attacker prevents the **defender** from moving into a space by using her or his body as a barrier.

Contact

The rules of netball do not allow any **contact** between players. Players must be careful not to contact another player at any time in the game.

The red Goal Shooter is holding a space in front of the Goal Keeper so that she can turn quickly to receive a pass from the Wing Attack.

NETBALL FACTS

It is important that beginners or young players try playing in all the different positions. This gives players a good range of attacking and defending skills. It also helps give players a better understanding of the game. As players improve, they can start to specialize. Most international players are able to play at least two different positions well.

Defending

A s soon as a team loses possession of the ball, everyone on that team must start to defend. The team without the ball must try to win it back from their opponents before they score. This takes a lot of hard work, concentration and determination. All of the players must use a range of defensive skills to try to retrieve the ball.

Intercepting

The aim of all **defending** is to try to win the ball. When a player catches a ball that was meant for an opponent it is called an **interception**. A **defender** must move quickly and at the right time to tip or catch the ball. The defenders still have to remain in their own playing areas on the court.

This Wing Defence is in a good position to mark the Wing Attack.

An interception followed by a fast attack back down the court looks really good. Sometimes players get too excited after making an interception. When this happens mistakes are made and the ball is lost to the opposition. After an interception, players need to stay calm and keep control of the ball.

Defending a pass

When a player has the ball, the defender tries to make it hard for the player to make a good pass. The defender must be 0.9 m (3 ft) away from the player's landing foot when defending. The defender can do two things: reach out in front of the player to mark the ball *or* jump to intercept the pass. The defender must watch the ball and jump at the right time.

Marking a player

Marking a player without the ball takes a lot of awareness. The defender must try to stay close to the attacker and shadow her or his movements. This makes it hard for the attacker to break free and receive a pass. The defender must also watch the ball in case a pass is made. If so the defender can try to intercept the pass.

Defending a shot

Defending a shot is like defending a pass. The difference is that with a shot you know where the target is. This is a special skill for the Goal Keepers and Goal Defences to practise. As when defending a pass, defenders must be 0.9 m (3 ft) away from the **shooter's** landing foot. Defenders can either lean to cover the ball from the front, side or behind, or jump to intercept the shot. The aim of both actions is to disrupt the opponent's shooting action. Good balance is needed to hold a reach position. Jumping to intercept requires timing and jumping ability.

Contact

Defenders must be careful not to come into **contact** with their opponent at any time. If they do, the **umpire** may give the opposition the ball and they could have the chance to score!

Liz Ellis of Australia jumping to defend a shot.

Playing a match

To play a netball match you need a court, two teams and two **umpires**.

Duration

Usually a netball match is made up of four **quarters** of 15 minutes each. At the end of each quarter there is a short interval. The interval at the end of the first and third quarters lasts three minutes and the half-time interval lasts five minutes. After each quarter the teams change ends. In junior matches or in tournaments, shorter games are often played in two halves.

The teams

Each team has a captain. Before a match the two captains toss a coin. The winner can decide to have first **centre pass** or decide which way to shoot. The captain must also notify the umpires and opposing team of any changes in position or **substitutions**.

The current England coach, Liz Broomhead, talks to players during an interval.

Coach

Most teams also have a coach. The role of the coach is to prepare players for matches and to give them advice about how to play the game. During the intervals in the game, the coach can advise players on what to do in the next quarter. A coach is not allowed to shout instructions to players during the game.

Umpires

There are two umpires who control the game. The umpires' job is to ensure everyone plays by the rules of the game. They are also responsible for the safety of players. During the game the umpires stay on opposite sides of the court. They each control half the court, normally the half to their right. They also control the whole of the nearest sideline and the goal line behind their half of the court.

Starting a game

The game is started with a centre pass. Before the whistle is blown to start the game, players must be in specific areas, as shown in the diagram. When the whistle is blown the Wing Attack, Goal Attack, Wing Defence and Goal Defence can move into the centre third. The centre pass must be received or touched by a player landing in the centre third.

Other officials

In important matches there will be two scorers and one timekeeper as well as umpires. The scorers' jobs are to record the centre passes, record each **goal** and keep a record of unsuccessful shots. The timekeeper's job is to time the quarters. Any time for stoppage is added so that a full 15 minutes is played in each quarter. Sometimes the umpires have to do all these jobs and are kept very busy!

SAFETY FIRST

Before a match starts, umpires must check that the court is safe to play on. They also check that players have short fingernails and are not wearing any jewellery. If this is not done, players could hurt themselves or other players.

This shows the players in the correct position for the start of play. Players must be in these positions before a centre pass can be made.

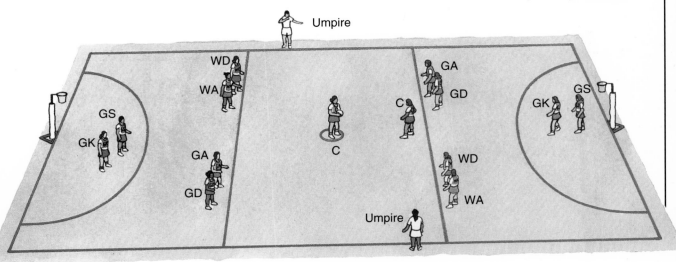

Rules of the game

There are various rules about the different aspects of the game. The full set of rules is laid out in a rule book. Some important rules are explained here.

Substitutions

A **substitution** takes place when one player leaves the court and is replaced by another player. Each team is allowed three substitutions in a game. Substitutions can only be made during one of the intervals, except when a player is injured. When this happens a substitution can be made during a **quarter**. Players already on court can change position during an interval or after an injury.

Breaking the rules

There are many different rules that players must follow. When a player breaks a rule the **umpire** will blow the whistle to stop the game and award one of the following.

A **penalty pass** is given when a player **contacts** or obstructs another player. Obstruction is when a player is too close when **defending a player** with the ball. The penalty pass is taken from the spot where the rule was broken. The player who committed the offence must stand beside the player taking the penalty pass until the ball has been released. If a player contacts or obstructs a player in the **goal circle** then a **penalty pass or shot** is given. This means the **shooter** can choose either to shoot or pass.

Here a penalty pass is being taken by the Goal Keeper. The Goal Shooter is the player who committed the offence, so is standing next to the Goal Keeper.

A **throw-in** is awarded to the opposing team when the ball goes out of court. A throw-in is a pass taken from outside the court, close to the line. The umpire shouts 'play' and the player must then release the ball before stepping on to court.

A **toss-up** is usually awarded when two players break a rule at the same time. The players must face each other 0.9 m (3 ft) apart with hands by their sides. The umpire blows the whistle and at the same time tosses the ball up in between the players. Whoever snatches the ball can then pass it on to a team mate.

A **free pass** is given when any other rule is broken. One example is when a player goes **offside.** This is when a player goes outside the correct playing area for that position. This may seem like a lot of rules to remember but players soon learn them just by playing!

This umpire is taking a toss-up between two players.

Training

To be well prepared for matches, players and teams must train regularly. Most teams will train together at least once a week. The type of training depends on the age and ability of the players.

Skills

Teams that have young or less experienced players may spend a lot of time practising the basic skills. The coach will set up a series of **drills** or practices. These are to help players improve a particular skill, such as passing. To encourage young players to practise the basic skills, many netball associations have skill awards. Players must successfully complete certain tests to gain an award.

Tactics

More experienced players will still practise these basic skills but spend more time on **tactics**. A tactic is a special plan of attack or defence. Teams may use a certain tactic to outwit the opposition. A tactic may include a set play. This is when the players use a particular series of movements that they have practised before. Many teams use set plays to work the ball from the **centre pass** towards the **goal circle**.

These young netballers are doing a passing drill in a circle.

22

Fitness training

Players must ensure that they are fit enough to play. This means spending time fitness training. All players need a good basic level of fitness. This involves the four Ss: stamina, strength, speed and suppleness. Stamina is the ability to keep going until the end of the game. Strength is important for passing and jumping. Speed helps players to move around the court quickly. Suppleness is the ability to stretch. Once players have a good basic level of fitness, they can start to concentrate on the areas of fitness most important for their position.

To be the best in the world, teams must try to be more skilful and better prepared than their opponents. To do this, many of the top international teams now have help from people called **sport scientists**. They can give advice on areas such as diet, technique and fitness training. They can also help players prepare mentally for competition. It takes a lot of hard work and dedication to play international netball.

NETBALL FACTS

The AENA has created a set of skill awards for players. There are three levels of awards: 1 star, 2 star and 3 star. Players obtain marks through performing a series of tests. These include running, ball handling, throwing and movement skills. Successful players receive a badge or certificate. A similar scheme has recently been developed for players with learning difficulties.

The England squad for the 1994 Test Series against South Africa.

Competition

Most young people learn to play netball at school. Others start by joining the junior section of a local club. Many adults become interested in netball and join a club. If you want to find out about your nearest club, you should contact your netball association for advice.

This young player is under pressure with two players defending the pass.

Competition

Teams can play in different types of competitions. There are leagues, tournaments and cup competitions. Leagues are played over a season. Tournaments are played over a day or more. In cup competitions, teams are knocked out when they lose. At junior levels, teams are divided into age groups to make the competition fair.

Teams that do well in local competitions can go on to compete in regional competitions. If they do well in those, they can go on to play in national competitions. Here they will meet the best teams in the country.

Individual players can also go on to play at higher levels. Good players can be selected to play for their area or county. If good enough, they may then be chosen to play for their region and even their country. This is many young players' dream!

Inter-County Tournament

In England, one of the big events of the year is the Inter-County Tournament. The main events are the under-21 and senior matches. Normally over 50 counties play in the two-day tournament. The weekend finishes with an under-21 final and then the senior final. There are a lot of tired netball players at the end but it is great fun!

National teams

Most countries have junior as well as senior national teams. In England, teams are currently selected for under-16, under-18 and under-21 age groups. This gives young players a chance to play in international matches and helps prepare players for the senior team. To reach the senior team you have to be the best. The highlight of a netball career must be to play in the World Championship. Teams from many different countries compete to find out who is the best in the world.

Birmingham v. East Essex in an Inter-County Tournament.

Famous teams

Australia have been the netball world champions since the 1991 World Championship in Sydney, Australia. In the final, Australia beat rivals New Zealand by only one **goal**, 53–52. It was a really exciting match watched by 10,000 people. In the 1995 World Championship, Australia beat South Africa in the final by 68 goals to 48. It was a great achievement for the South African team to reach the final. For 21 years they had not been allowed to compete in international netball for political reasons. This was their first World Championship since returning to international competition in 1994.

Australia

So why is the Australian team so good? Part of the reason is that Australia has a good system for helping talented young players. They are invited to go and live and train at special schools of sport. These are called Institutes of Sport. Here players receive expert coaching and training as well as help from **sport scientists**. They get free accommodation and kit but must work or study part-time. By the time they leave, they have learnt a lot and have become much better players.

The Australian team celebrates winning the 1995 World Championships.

New Zealand defenders Belinda Blair and Bernice Mene in action.

The 1995 World Championship

In the 1995 World Championship, New Zealand defeated England by 60 goals to 31 to take third place. The New Zealand team had hoped to reclaim the World Championship title from Australia but it was not to be. They were beaten by South Africa by one goal in the first round. This meant that they came up against Australia in the second round and were beaten by one goal again: 45–44. England retained fourth position by beating all the Caribbean teams. Wales finished up in 17th place, Northern Ireland in 18th place and Scotland in 22nd place. As standards at the World Championship improve it gets harder to stay amongst the top countries.

The Cook Islands

Other teams may not be in the top few teams but are quite famous for other reasons. The Cook Islands team is always a favourite with the crowd. During a walk-on before a match they wear beautiful flowers in their hair. This is traditional in their country in the South Pacific. They are also popular with the other teams. They are well known for playing the guitar, singing and dancing at official ceremonies and dinners. They are also very good at netball!

NETBALL FACTS

Although netball started in the USA, for many years they did not have an international team. The 1995 World Championship was the first time the USA was entered. This was nearly 100 years after the game started there!

Famous faces

M any netball players become famous in their own country. To become world-famous, players have to be really special.

Kendra Slawinski

One English player who has achieved fame both in England and in the world is Kendra Slawinski. Kendra first played for England at under-18 level in 1980. She was selected for the senior England squad in 1982 and was captain from 1989 until her retirement in 1995. She played her last match against the Cook Islands in Manchester in November 1995. This was her 128th international netball match and it set a record that is now in the *Guinness Book of Records*. She has also appeared twice on the television sports quiz programme 'A Question of Sport'. This has helped give netball the extra publicity it needs in the UK.

Kendra Slawinsk in action for Bedfordshire County.

Sandra Edge

Sandra Edge of New Zealand became famous as one of the best **centre court players** in the world. She has even been seen in television advertisements in New Zealand. Netball gets much better coverage in New Zealand and Australia than in Europe.

Michelle Feilke

Other players have also become famous throughout the world. Michelle Feilke has been captain of Australia since 1989 and has two World Championship gold medals. She usually plays Goal Defence but can also play Goal Keeper. When on court she works extremely hard throughout the game. She is an inspiration to all her team.

Sandra Edge is a famous player from New Zealand.

NETBALL FACTS

In the Queen's 1996 New Year's Honour list, Kendra Slawinski was awarded an OBE. This stands for Officer of the Order of the British Empire. This was awarded for services to netball, and it was a magnificent achievement for Kendra.

Irene Van Dyk

In the 1995 World Tournament, some new players became famous. Irene Van Dyk of South Africa got a lot of attention from the press. Her accurate shooting and excellent movement skills played a big part in South Africa's success.

All these players have worked hard for many years to be the best at the sport they love. Who knows – maybe you could become a world-famous netball player!

Glossary

attacking Any movements made by players while their team is in possession of the ball, moving towards their goal end to score.

amateur Players who are not paid to take part in the sport.

bounce pass A low-level pass that is used over short distances. The ball is pushed towards the ground with either one or two hands.

centre circle This is in the centre of the court and is 0.9 m (3 ft) in diameter. This is where the centre pass is taken from.

centre court players The players who play mainly in the centre third, i.e. Wing Attack, Centre and Wing Defence.

centre pass At the start of the game, at the start of each quarter or after each goal is scored, the game is restarted by a centre pass. The centre pass is taken by the Centre from the centre circle and alternates between the two teams throughout the game.

chest pass A short, two-handed pass from the chest of the thrower to the chest of the receiver.

contact When a player runs into or bumps another. It is an offence.

defenders The two main defenders, i.e. Goal Keeper and Goal Defence. However, when the opposition have the ball then everyone becomes a defender.

defending Any movements made by players when their team is not in possession of the ball.

drills Practices to help players improve their playing skills.

feint dodge A player pretends to move in one direction but suddenly runs in the other direction.

follow-through The extension of the arms, hands and fingers as a thrower releases the ball. This helps give the ball direction.

free pass The penalty awarded for individual offences such as footwork and offside.

getting free Players attempt to move into a position where they can receive the ball.

goal When the ball goes through the ring, having been shot by the Goal Shooter or Goal Attack.

goal circle The area inside the semi-circle that is 4.9 m (16 ft) away from the goal post.

goal post A post 3.05 m (10 ft) high with a metal hoop of 380 mm (15 in) in diameter at the top. There is one goal post at each end of the court.

holding a space When a player prevents an opponent from moving into a space by using her or his body as a barrier.

interception When a player catches or tips a ball that was meant for an opponent.

marking a player Staying close to an opponent and shadowing her or his movements.

offside When a player enters an area of the court outside the correct area for that playing position.

penalty pass Awarded when a player contacts or obstructs an opponent.

penalty pass or shot Awarded when a defender contacts or obstructs a shooter inside the goal circle.

playing bibs Worn by each player in a game to indicate their playing position. They show the letters of the playing position e.g. GS (Goal Shooter) or GK (Goal Keeper).

quarters The four 15-minute periods in a full match.

shooters The players who are allowed to shoot i.e. the Goal Shooter and Goal Attack.

shoulder pass A fast, hard pass that is used over long distances. It is a one-handed pass and the ball is thrown from shoulder or head height.

sport scientists Scientists who can give players and coaches advice on how to prepare mentally and/or physically for competition.

substitution When one player leaves the court and is replaced by another.

tactic A special plan of attack or defence.

throw-in Awarded to the opposing team when the ball goes out of court.

toss-up Usually awarded when two players break a rule at the same time or the umpire is unable to make a decision. The umpire restarts the game by tossing the ball up between the two players who stand facing each other 0.9m (3ft) apart.

transverse lines The two lines that divide the court into thirds.

umpires Two officials who control the game and ensure players abide by the rules.

Index

Numbers in plain type (4) refer to the text. Numbers in italic type (*4*) refer to a caption.